ROSA PARKS
AND THE MONTGOMERY BUS BOYCOTT

By Karen Latchana Kenney

Content Consultant
Françoise N. Hamlin
Departments of Africana Studies & History
Brown University

Core Library

An Imprint of Abdo Publishing
abdopublishing.com

abdopublishing.com

Published by Abdo Publishing, a division of ABDO, PO Box 398166, Minneapolis, Minnesota 55439. Copyright © 2016 by Abdo Consulting Group, Inc. International copyrights reserved in all countries. No part of this book may be reproduced in any form without written permission from the publisher. Core Library™ is a trademark and logo of Abdo Publishing.

Printed in the United States of America, North Mankato, Minnesota

032015
092015

Cover Photo: Gene Herrick/AP Images
Interior Photos: Gene Herrick/AP Images, 1, 26, 37, 43, 45; Montgomery County Sheriff's Office/AP Images, 4; The National Archives, 7; North Wind Picture Archives, 10; AP Images, 13; Atlanta Journal-Constitution/AP Images, 15; Michael J. Samojeden/AP Images, 18; Arthur Rothstein/Library of Congress, 21 (left); Marion Post Wolcott/Library of Congress, 21 (right); Everett Collection/Newscom, 23; Gene Herrick/AP Images/© 1955 Dr. Martin Luther King, Jr. © renewed 1983 Coretta Scott King, 30; Bettmann/Corbis, 32; Bettmann/Corbis/© 1956 Dr. Martin Luther King, Jr. © renewed 1984 Coretta Scott King, 34, 39

Editor: Mirella Miller
Series Designer: Becky Daum

Library of Congress Control Number: 2015931183

Cataloging-in-Publication Data
Kenney, Karen Latchana.
 Rosa Parks and the Montgomery Bus Boycott / Karen Latchana Kenney.
   p. cm. -- (Stories of the civil rights movement)
Includes bibliographical references and index.
ISBN 978-1-62403-884-6
1. Montgomery Bus Boycott, Montgomery, Ala., 1955-1956--Juvenile literature. 2. African Americans--Civil rights--Alabama--Montgomery--History--20th century--Juvenile literature. 3. Segregation in transportation--Alabama--Montgomery--History--20th century--Juvenile literature. 3. Civil rights movements--Alabama--Montgomery--History--20th century--Juvenile literature. I. Title.
323--dc23
                                        2015931183

CONTENTS

CHAPTER ONE
Time for Change 4

CHAPTER TWO
Separate and Unequal 10

CHAPTER THREE
Becoming a Leader 18

CHAPTER FOUR
The Bus Boycott 26

CHAPTER FIVE
A Change for Equality 34

Snapshot of Rosa Parks's Arrest 42

Stop and Think 44

Glossary 46

Learn More 47

Index 48

About the Author 48

TIME FOR CHANGE

I t was the end of a workday on December 1, 1955—a regular day for seamstress Rosa Parks. This African-American woman and local civil rights activist was on her way home during rush hour in Montgomery, Alabama. She rode the bus, and that meant following the city's bus segregation laws.

At that time, the South was segregated—drinking fountains, public bathrooms, restaurants, waiting

This booking photo shows Rosa Parks after her arrest on December 1, 1955.

rooms, trains, and much more. State laws prevented African Americans and whites from mixing. The laws limited the rights of African Americans. They were treated as second-class citizens by whites.

In Montgomery, the first ten seats of a bus were reserved for white passengers. Other states had laws about bus segregation, too, including Arkansas, Florida, Georgia, Louisiana, Mississippi, Oklahoma, Tennessee, and Texas. African Americans had to sit at the back of the bus and could not enter through the front door. On December 1, Parks

CIVIL RIGHTS VOICES
Rosa Parks

When I made that decision, I knew I had the strength of my ancestors with me.
A pioneer in the civil rights movement, Rosa Parks was born in 1913 in Tuskegee, Alabama. She became an activist in Montgomery in the 1940s. Her actions sparked the Montgomery Bus Boycott. After the boycott, Parks moved to Detroit, Michigan. She continued to work for civil rights. She died in Detroit in 2005 at the age of 92.

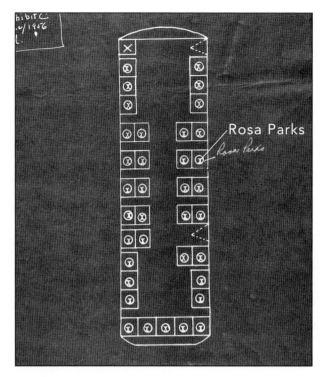

Segregated Bus Seating

This diagram shows where Parks sat in the bus when she was arrested in 1955. How does seeing this seating diagram help you understand the description of Parks's protest? Does it help you understand how African Americans may have felt obeying the segregation laws at the time?

bought her ticket, boarded through the back door, and sat just behind the white section.

After three stops, more white people boarded the bus. The white section filled up, and one white man had no place to sit. Bus drivers had a lot of power and carried guns. The bus driver that day was a white man named James F. Blake. He was known by people in the city for being a bigot, which is a person who dislikes members of a particular group. He often played a cruel trick on African-American passengers. He would give them their tickets and then drive off before they had time to board at the back door.

On that evening, Blake approached the row where Parks sat. African-American passengers occupied all four seats in the row. Blake told them, "Move, y'all, I want those two seats." At first no one moved. Silence gripped the packed bus. The bus driver insisted again, ordering, "Y'all better make it light on yourselves and let me have those seats." Slowly the three other passengers in Parks's row stood up and moved to the back of the bus. All the colored seats were now taken. Parks remained seated, moving instead to the seat by the window. She was not angry, but she was determined. This was an opportunity— her chance to take a stand against unfair laws and treatment of African Americans.

The bus driver asked Parks if she too was going to move. When Parks told him she would not move, Blake said he would have her arrested. Parks simply responded, "You may do that."

Aftermath of the Arrest

With her resulting arrest, Parks sparked the Montgomery Bus Boycott. Her quiet, peaceful action spoke loudly. It echoed across the country. The boycott led to more nonviolent direct action protests and eventual legislative wins in the civil rights movement of the United States.

Previous Problems

Parks had issues with James F. Blake, the bus driver, before. In 1943 Parks tried to board Blake's bus from the front door. African Americans had to buy their tickets at the front. Then they had to exit the bus and board through the back door. But the bus was full, and Parks could not enter through the rear door. Parks insisted on boarding at the front. Blake told Parks to get off his bus. When she refused, he began pushing her. Parks finally exited by herself, warning Blake not to hit her. She did not board his bus again until December 1, 1955.

CHAPTER TWO

SEPARATE AND UNEQUAL

Having few rights was nothing new to African Americans. African Americans had fought battles to gain equal rights for centuries. Since 1619 Africans had been forced into slavery by whites in the American colonies. They were forced to work unpaid on plantations. Their labor made their owners incredibly wealthy and supported the national economy.

Many slaves in the South were forced to pick cotton or other crops.

As the colonies grew and became a united country, leaders debated the issue of slavery. The Southern states feared their farms would collapse without free labor. By the mid-1800s, many in the North wanted slavery to be abolished. The issue sparked the American Civil War (1861–1865), which nearly tore the country apart. In 1865 the North won the American Civil War. The US government passed the Thirteenth Amendment, freeing all slaves and legally ending slavery. Slavery had become illegal, but racial prejudice had not disappeared.

The Ku Klux Klan

Six American Civil War veterans from the South formed the Ku Klux Klan in 1866. It began in Tennessee and soon spread to other states. Its members wore white robes and hats. Klan members beat and murdered African Americans. They burned African-American churches. Their victims were men and women, young and old. States protected Klan members by rarely arresting them for their crimes.

Public spaces, including waiting spaces, were segregated for many years.

Racial Segregation

In 1875 the federal government passed a civil rights act, which forbade racial discrimination in public spaces. Its goal was to protect the rights of African Americans. But in 1883, the US Supreme Court declared the law unconstitutional. The court decided the federal government had the right to regulate states, but the 1875 law aimed to control individuals, which made it unconstitutional. The US Supreme Court ruled in favor of segregation in 1896. The court ruled that separate facilities for African Americans and whites were legal as long as they were equal. But African-American facilities were never as good as white facilities.

This was around the time when many local and state lawmakers passed Jim Crow laws in the United States. Jim Crow laws enforced racial segregation. Businesses and public facilities were separated between "colored" (for African Americans) and whites. Signs labeled "colored" or "whites only" showed white and African-American people where they could and could not go.

Jim Crow also set certain social codes for African Americans. They were not written in law. But African Americans knew they might be hurt or killed by whites if they went against these social codes. One code was that African Americans and whites could not eat together. Another was that African Americans had to

People openly protested against Jim Crow laws, which were designed to humiliate and oppress African Americans.

call white people by their formal names, such as Mr. Hansen. Whites called African Americans by their first names.

Alabama's Segregation

At the time of Mrs. Parks's arrest in Montgomery, Alabama, segregation was part of life. In almost every way, African Americans and whites lived separate

There was a history of protest on public transportation. From 1900 to 1907, African Americans boycotted segregated streetcars in 27 cities in Alabama. One of those cities was Montgomery. One streetcar company did not segregate their riders for a short while. Then segregation began again.

social lives. Very few African Americans were registered to vote. This was because of certain laws, such as a voting tax. Many African Americans lived in poverty and could not afford the tax. African Americans were also often denied registration to vote. By restricting African-American voters, white politicians controlled the local government. They represented white needs and ignored those of African Americans.

Segregation was even more visible on public buses. It was one of the few facilities that both African Americans and whites used, and it made the physical separation between them more obvious.

Things were changing in the country, though. The courts were moving toward ending segregation. In 1954 the US Supreme Court ruling on *Brown v. Board of Education* was delivered. It said that segregation in schools was unconstitutional. By 1955 the African-American community in Montgomery was ready for a boycott. Segregation had to go.

FURTHER EVIDENCE

This chapter covered the Jim Crow laws of the South. It explained how they affected African Americans. What are some of the main points about the laws? What evidence supports these points? Visit the website at the link below. It provides the text of some Jim Crow laws. Do the specific laws help you better understand how African Americans were treated? Write a few sentences explaining your thoughts.

Jim Crow Laws

mycorelibrary.com/montgomery-bus-boycott

CHAPTER THREE

BECOMING A LEADER

Standing up for oneself during the early 1900s could be dangerous. It could result in beatings, houses being burned down, or murder. But standing up for herself was something Rosa Parks learned to do from a young age.

Rosa was born in Tuskegee, Alabama, on February 4, 1913. She grew up with her mother,

Parks's family encouraged a strong sense of African-American pride throughout Parks's life.

brother, and grandparents. Her grandparents were former slaves.

A Good Education

Education was very important to Rosa's mother, who was a schoolteacher. Her mother taught Rosa to read before she began school.

Jim Crow laws meant that Rosa went to African-American schools. The school year only lasted five to six months. Then the children helped their families work in the fields. White schools were open for nine months. They had nice brick buildings. White children rode buses to school. African-American children had to walk to school. The government gave less funding to African-American schools. Their schools were small and had few supplies. The African-American community gave what they could to help out. Rosa saw that the schools were not equal.

At 11 years old, Rosa went to school in Montgomery. She continued her education at Miss White's school for African-American girls. Some white

Alabama's Segregated Schools
Take a look at these two photographs of schools in Alabama during the 1930s. The image on the left shows an African-American school held in a church. The image on the right shows a white classroom. After reading about Parks's experiences at school, what do these photographs tell you about Alabama's segregated schools? How are they different? How are the schools similar? Which looks like a better school to attend?

kids threatened Rosa while she was in the city. She stood up for herself and did not allow them to bully her. Rosa continued school through the eleventh grade.

Getting Involved

Parks met her future husband Raymond in 1931. Raymond fought against racism. He was involved with a case involving nine young African-American boys. They were called the Scottsboro Boys. Raymond

Scottsboro Boys

Nine African-American boys, ranging in age from 12 to 19, had been riding the trains to find work. A fight broke out with some white youths. Armed men took the African-American boys to jail. Two white girls dressed in boys' clothing were among them. The girls told the sheriff that the African-American boys had raped them, although this was not true. Each of the nine boys spent between six and nineteen years in jail.

worked to help free the young men, although it was very dangerous. Parks greatly admired Raymond's work and activism. They married in 1932.

In 1943 Parks became involved in the civil rights movement too. She joined the National Association for the Advancement of Colored People (NAACP) in Montgomery. Its members discussed ways to help the African-American community. She was one of two women in the organization. There she worked with E. D. Nixon. He would become an important partner to Parks in her activism.

Future Supreme Court justice Thurgood Marshall, right, attends an NAACP meeting in 1956.

Being involved with the NAACP was very dangerous at that time. The group tried to expose lynchers. These mobs of white people attacked and murdered African Americans. The NAACP also tried to use the law to get justice for African-American victims of white violence. It was hard work without much reward. But this work helped to generate the mass movement for civil rights.

In the summer of 1955, Parks attended a two-week session at the Highlander Folk School in Tennessee. Parks met other leaders in the movement. There she learned about ways to fight segregation in the South.

The Highlander Folk School

Established in 1932 near Monteagle, Tennessee, the Highlander Folk School focused on solving societal problems and proposing solutions. It held workshops that lasted from two days to eight weeks. The school brought leaders from many cultures and backgrounds together at its workshops. Many African-American and white activists in the civil rights movement attended the school.

Early Protests

Parks was not the first person to protest bus segregation. Many had paved the way for her. In 1944 Viola White refused to give up her seat in Montgomery. She was beaten and arrested. In 1950 veteran Hilliard Brooks, after giving the driver his ticket, refused to exit the bus just to enter again through the rear door. A police officer shot and killed Brooks. The police officer was not punished.

In 1955 the Montgomery NAACP was trying to find a test case to challenge bus segregation. A test case is one that is appealed until it reaches the US Supreme Court. The Supreme Court justices decide whether the facts in the case follow or go against the US Constitution. By the time of Parks's arrest in December, the NAACP was ready. This would be the test case they had waited for.

EXPLORE ONLINE

This chapter focuses on Parks's early involvement in civil rights issues. It also mentions the Highlander Folk School. The website below explains more about this school. As you know, every source is different. How is the information given on the website different from the information in this chapter? What information is the same? How do the two sources present information differently? What can you learn from this website?

Highlander Folk School
mycorelibrary.com/montgomery-bus-boycott

CHAPTER FOUR

THE BUS BOYCOTT

That December day—when Parks refused to give up her seat—had a bigger effect than she could have ever imagined. She had not planned on being arrested, let alone setting an entire movement into motion. It was the beginning of change. And that kind of change is never easy.

Parks arrives at an Alabama court on March 19, 1956, with E. D. Nixon.

After two policemen arrested Parks, they took her to the city hall jail. E. D. Nixon came to the jail. Nixon paid the $100 bail and the police released Parks.

Back at the Parks's apartment, they discussed the arrest. Nixon suggested they use the arrest to challenge segregation. He said the struggle would be long and difficult, but worth it in the end.

A One-Day Boycott

News of Parks's arrest spread quickly. Many in the African-American community were frustrated. They were ready to do something. The talk turned to boycott. The Women's Political Council (WPC) printed leaflets asking African Americans to stay off the buses on the day of Parks's trial.

The next morning, Nixon called Reverend Martin Luther King Jr. and other prominent African-American men in the city. He asked for their support in protesting segregation. King agreed and offered his church for the first boycott meeting. Nixon also gave the leaflet to a reporter, who put it on the front page of the *Montgomery Advertiser.* Now everyone knew to boycott the buses on December 5.

On the day of Parks' trial African Americans walking to work and school filled the sidewalks. News of the boycott had spread and participation was higher than expected.

Many people came to the court that morning. They wanted to show support for Parks. In just 30 minutes, she was found guilty of breaking state law. The judge fined her $14.

CIVIL RIGHTS VOICES
Martin Luther King Jr.

If we are wrong, the Supreme Court of this nation is wrong. If we are wrong, the Constitution of the United States is wrong. . . . If we are wrong, justice is a lie.

Martin Luther King Jr. became a well-known leader of the civil rights movement. He gave his speech about the boycott four days after Parks's arrest. King supported nonviolent protest as a way for African Americans to gain their civil rights. He continued leading the movement until his death in 1968.

King gives his speech at Holt Street Baptist Church to an overflow crowd.

The Boycott Goes On

The night after Parks's trial, close to 15,000 African Americans gathered at the Holt Street Baptist Church. People filled the streets around the church. They were informed on what to do next. First E. D. Nixon spoke to the crowd. He told them change would come at a price. It would be a hard and long struggle, but it needed to happen. Then it was Reverend King's turn. He had not prepared a speech. Yet the one he delivered moved the crowd. When he was finished, everyone stood, cheered, and clapped. Then they voted to continue the boycott. They would not stop until bus segregation ended.

That night they also formed the Montgomery Improvement Association (MIA). This group would manage and lead the boycott. The MIA would later be important in other civil rights protests.

At the beginning, the MIA had some simple demands for the bus companies. African Americans did not want to have to move for white

The Carpool System

To make the boycott work, its leaders helped African Americans get to and from work. The MIA's carpool system was highly organized. Every day approximately 300 cars drove the carpool's passengers. The service operated from 5:00 a.m. to 8:00 p.m. Its volunteer drivers, both African Americans and whites, took big risks by being in the carpool.

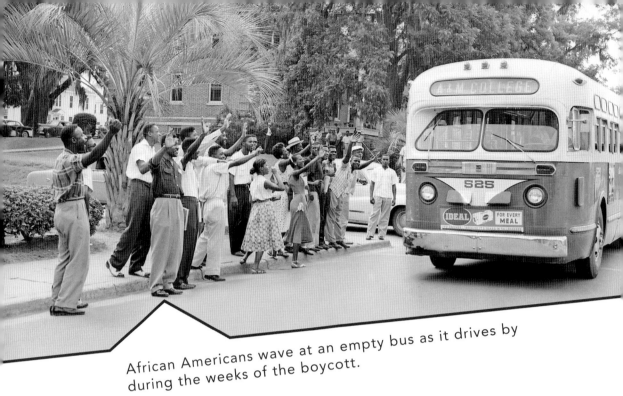

African Americans wave at an empty bus as it drives by during the weeks of the boycott.

passengers. They wanted African Americans to be treated fairly. And they wanted the companies to hire some African-American drivers. The bus companies did not budge. Neither did the protesters. It made the boycott stronger.

The MIA stressed that the boycott remain peaceful. Whites constantly harassed carpool drivers and riders. The protesters did not react with violence. The boycotters' peaceful protest showed they were committed and dedicated. Their protest was about equality.

The day after Parks's arrest, more than 52,000 leaflets were printed by the WPC and given out to churches, stores, restaurants, and African-American homes. Jo Ann Gibson Robinson was president of the WPC. She quickly wrote the notice, made copies, and helped get the leaflets out:

> *This is for Monday, December 5, 1955. Another Negro woman has been arrested and thrown into jail because she refused to get up out of her seat on the bus for a white person to sit down. . . . This has to be stopped. . . . We are, therefore, asking every Negro to stay off the buses Monday in protest of the arrest and trial. Don't ride the buses to work, to town, to school, or anywhere on Monday. . . . If you work, take a cab or walk. But please, children and grownups, don't ride the bus at all on Monday. Please stay off of all buses, Monday.*

Source: Jo Ann Gibson Robinson. The Montgomery Bus Boycott and the Women Who Started It. *Knoxville, TN: The University of Tennessee Press, 1987. Print. 45–46.*

What's the Big Idea?

Take a close look at the text of this leaflet. What does it say about how the WPC felt about the arrest? Notice the term "Negro," which was used to describe an African-American person at the time. Pick out two details the author uses to make her point. What do you notice about how she asks people in the African-American community to stay off the buses?

A CHANGE FOR EQUALITY

The boycott lasted for 381 days. Parks lost her job early in the protest. Her husband was forced to quit his job. Whites tried to break the boycott any way they could. Rotten food, rocks, and urine were thrown at those walking. The police gave carpool drivers dozens of tickets for no reason. Cars were damaged too. Gas tanks were filled with sugar. Brakes were disconnected. And many people's homes were

King speaks out after a bomb damaged his home in 1956.

damaged. Then Reverend King's home was bombed on January 30, 1956. No one was hurt, but the message was clear. Many whites wanted things to go back to the way they were.

The Montgomery White Citizen's Council (WCC) formed to respond to the boycott. Many whites did not want their way of life to change. Changing bus segregation would be the start of many other changes.

The boycott showed the power African Americans had when united for a cause. It meant that whites would eventually lose their dominating position in

Crowds gather outside the Montgomery Jail in 1956 to boycott bus segregation.

southern society. On February 10, more than 10,000 people gathered at a WCC meeting. The group gained power in the city, and its members included many powerful men, such as bank presidents, the mayor of Montgomery, and the police chief. It became dangerous for whites to interact with African Americans. Whites who were involved with the protest were in danger. Many were attacked or lost their jobs. It was a scary time in Montgomery.

Going to Court

The way to change was through the courts. Parks's case could not be appealed to higher courts because of clerical error. On February 1, African-American leaders filed a federal case to challenge bus segregation. This was the *Browder v. Gayle* case. Its plaintiffs were Aurelia Browder, Susie McDonald, Claudette Colvin, and Mary Louise Smith. They were all African-American women who had been mistreated while using the public bus system in Montgomery.

Shortly after, the city filed a case too. They found an old law, from a 1903 streetcar boycott, that made boycotts illegal. So the city issued warrants for 89 civil rights leaders, including Rosa Parks

Work in Detroit

In 1957, Parks moved to Detroit, Michigan, with her husband and mother. From 1965 to 1988, she worked as an assistant to US Representative John Conyers Jr. She was given several awards for her work in the civil rights movement. Parks died at the age of 92 on October 24, 2005.

King rides the bus in December after the bus boycott victory.

and Reverend King. The arrests made national news. Photographers and reporters came from around the country. Many newspapers supported the boycotters.

The *Browder v. Gayle* case made its way to the US Supreme Court. A lower court decided on June 5, 1956, that bus segregation was illegal. The Supreme Court agreed with this decision on November 13. But the city of Montgomery still did not agree with the decision.

After the Decision

It took another month for the decision to take effect. The city tried to have the decision reviewed again. But it did not work. On December 20, the city received the order to end bus segregation. King and other African-American leaders boarded the buses. They sat at the front. A little more than one year after the bus strike had begun, the boycott was finally over.

Violence against the black community continued. King's home was shot at. Four churches were bombed. Two civil rights leaders' homes and a gas station were bombed too. Bus service stopped for a few weeks.

The buses were no longer segregated. But the rest of Montgomery was. By the early 1960s, that changed. More direct action protests forced segregation laws to end in the city. It took Rosa Parks's courage to start that battle. It took her strength, along with that of many other leaders, to keep that battle moving toward victory.

The decision in the *Browder v. Gayle* case made history. It ended segregation on buses in Montgomery, Alabama. The following is from this case's decision:

> *We hold that the statutes and ordinances requiring segregation of the white and colored races on the motor buses of a common carrier of passengers in the City of Montgomery and its police jurisdiction violate the due process and equal protection of the law clauses of the Fourteenth Amendment to the Constitution of the United States.*

> *Source: "Browder v. Gayle (1956)." Dr. Quintard Taylor Jr. University of Washington, n.d. Web. Accessed February 5, 2015.*

Consider Your Audience

Review this passage closely. Why is it written that way? Consider how you would adapt it for a different audience, such as your parents or friends. Write a blog post conveying this same information for the new audience. How does your new approach differ from the original text and why?

Rosa Parks is arrested for refusing to give up her seat on a public bus. She is one of 89 civil rights leaders arrested for boycotting segregation in Montgomery.

Date

December 1, 1955

Key Players

Rosa Parks, E. D. Nixon, Martin Luther King Jr., the NAACP

What Happened

On December 1, 1955, Rosa Parks refused to give her seat to a white passenger on the bus. She was arrested. On December 5, 1955, African Americans stayed off the buses. It was the day of Parks's trial. She was found guilty. That night, the community voted to begin a bus boycott. The bus boycott continued for 381 days.

Impact

The boycott hurt the bus system. It showed that African Americans had the power to hurt the finances of businesses in the city. The boycott's legal win showed that the civil rights movement could change the laws in the United States. This resulted in fairer treatment of African Americans.

Why Do I Care?

The Montgomery Bus Boycott happened during the 1950s. It affected the legal rights of African Americans in the United States. But it was not only important to African Americans. It showed that all people should have equal rights. How do you think the bus boycott relates to you? What do you think the world might be like if the boycott had never happened? How might your life be affected?

Take a Stand

This book discusses how Rosa Parks participated in the Montgomery Bus Boycott. Do you think Parks should have given up her seat? Or do you agree with her decision? Many African Americans followed the laws for many years. They did not want to cause problems or be arrested. What would you have done in Parks's position? Write a short essay explaining your opinion. Make sure to give reasons for your opinion, and facts and details that support those reasons.

You Are There

This book discusses what it was like growing up during the Jim Crow era. Imagine you attend a segregated school. You see a bus filled with white children going to their school. How does it make you feel seeing them on the bus while you walk?

Say What?

Studying about the civil rights movement can mean learning a lot of new vocabulary. Find five words in this book that you have never heard before. Use a dictionary to find out what they mean. Then write the meanings in your own words, and use each word in a new sentence.

GLOSSARY

abolished
to formally put an end to a practice, such as slavery

activist
a person who campaigns for social change

boycott
to protest by refusing to buy or use goods and services

lynchers
a mob of people who murder someone and are rarely caught or punished

plaintiffs
people who bring legal action to the courts

plantations
large farms where crops are grown to be sold

prejudice
an unfair opinion about a person or a group of people based on race or other characteristics

racism
a belief that race defines certain values and traits of people, and that one race is more important than another

segregation
the practice of keeping different races apart from each other

unconstitutional
not in agreement with a constitution, particularly the US Constitution

LEARN MORE

Books

Hay, Jeff, Ed. *The Montgomery Bus Boycott.*
Farmington Hills, MI: Greenhaven Press, 2012.

Shea, Therese. *Rosa Parks.* New York: Britannica
Educational Publishing, 2015.

Watson, Stephanie. *Martin Luther King Jr. and
the March on Washington.* Minneapolis: Abdo
Publishing, 2016.

Websites

To learn more about Stories of the Civil Rights
Movement, visit **booklinks.abdopublishing.com**.
These links are routinely monitored and updated to
provide the most current information available.

Visit **mycorelibrary.com** for free additional tools for
teachers and students.

INDEX

Blake, James F., 8–9
Browder v. Gayle, 38–39, 41
Brown v. Board of Education, 17
bus segregation laws, 5–6, 7, 24–25, 31, 36, 38–39, 40, 41

carpool system, 31, 32, 35

Gray, Fred, 36

Highlander Folk School, 24, 25

Jim Crow laws, 14, 17, 20

King, Martin Luther, Jr., 28, 29, 31, 36, 39, 40

Montgomery, Alabama, 5–6, 15, 16, 17, 20, 22, 24, 36, 37, 38–41
Montgomery Bus Boycott, 6, 9
Montgomery Improvement Association (MIA), 31–32
Montgomery White Citizen's Council (WCC), 36–37

National Association for the Advancement of Colored People (NAACP), 22–23, 25

Nixon, E. D., 22, 28, 30

Parks, Raymond, 21–22, 35, 38
Parks, Rosa, 5–9, 15, 19–25, 27–30, 33, 35, 36, 38, 40

schools, 17, 20–21
Scottsboro Boys, 21, 22
segregation, 13–14, 15–17, 24, 28, 40
slavery, 11–12
Supreme Court, 13–14, 17, 25, 29, 39

Women's Political Council (WPC), 28, 33

ABOUT THE AUTHOR

Karen Latchana Kenney is the author of more than 100 books for children. She loves writing about civil rights heroes and issues. Kenney lives and works in Minneapolis, Minnesota.